'This tall spired town … a very brave place', enthused Samuel Pepys whilst visiting Salisbury in 1668, when the city was already more than 450 years old. Today the illustrious diarist's description remains valid: a lively, vibrant city dominated by a cathedral of exceptional beauty, topped by England's tallest spire. This Gothic masterpiece stands in the Close, a serene, timeless place where country meets city. A place of towering trees, glorious gardens, well-cut grass, bordered on two sides by the River Avon beyond a long line of elegant period houses.

On the other two sides of the Close lies a bustling city centre retaining much of its original medieval charac... fine churches, ha... and coaching inns. Twice weekly markets continue to be held in the central square. There is an excellent theatre, an attractive racecourse and an annual festival of growing international reputation.

North of the city lies Salisbury Plain and Stonehenge, to which the intrepid Samuel Pepys rode 8 miles (12.8km), with his horse led by a shepherd woman. Today the 5,000 year old neolithic monument has been designated a World Heritage Site. Its stones, as Samuel Pepys noted in his diary, 'as prodigious as any tales I ever heard of them and worth going the journey to see.'

the Chapter House together with the Cathedral School, once the Bishop's Palace, is much as Constable painted it in 1823.

History

At first glance Salisbury portrays the appearance of a traditional old English town – its ancient buildings left behind by the high tide of history – yet the city is an early example of a new town, purpose-built on a totally clear, level site: an embryonic Milton Keynes or Basildon. The gridded street plan, a medieval Manhattan, developed

LEFT **Bishop Richard Poore supervised the laying of five foundation stones on the site of the new cathedral on 28 April 1220, depicted here in this 20th-century stained glass window in the Cathedral.**

ABOVE **This characterful medieval face jug is to be found in the excellent Salibury and South Wiltshire Museum.**

BELOW **The ruins of the original town, bishop's palace and Norman castle, together with the foundations of the cathedral of Old Sarum can still be seen on high ground north of Salisbury.**

ABOVE Within a few years of the foundation of new Salisbury, the original town of Old Sarum fell into terminal decline. Turner's early 19th-century painting of the Cathedral from Old Sarum shows grass covered ruins inhabited solely by sheep and shepherds. Turner had been commissioned by the owner of nearby Stourhead to record local scenes. Today five of his paintings are in the Salisbury and South Wiltshire Museum.

around the new cathedral and the all-important market, following Bishop Richard Poore's momentous decision to move down into the valley in the early 13th century from the bleak, windswept heights of Old Sarum, one time prehistoric hillfort, which had contained the original town and cathedral established soon after the Norman Conquest. Standing on the site of Old Sarum today, particularly in winter, it is easy to appreciate why the clergy were so anxious to move to the greater comforts of the valley below. They took many of their priceless treasures with them, and some of these can now be seen in the Cathedral and in the Salisbury and South Wiltshire Museum. To this day the bishop continues to use the signature 'Sarum'.

Salisbury's prosperity in the Middle Ages came from the wool trade. By 1500 it was the fourth largest city in southern England. It continued to flourish in Tudor and Stuart times as a

ABOVE An angel holds the Coat of Arms of the University of Oxford on the wall of De Vaux House, where a short-lived college was established in 1261.

Myles Place, where the distinguished English historian, Sir Arthur Bryant, lived for a number of years, until his death in 1985 at the age of 86. Sir Nikolaus Pevsner described his home as 'the stateliest 18th-century house in the Close.' Bryant is best known for his perceptive biographies of Samuel Pepys and Charles II, together with a brilliant series of histories of the Napoleonic war and Regency eras. Knighted in 1954, his ashes are buried in the Cathedral, simply inscribed 'Historian of his country'.

fashionable place favoured by royalty, particularly James I, after whom The King's House is named, whilst Charles II was also a frequent visitor. This encouraged the development of many of Salisbury's most notable dwellings particularly in and around the Close.

A period of relative decline in the city's fortunes began in the 19th century. In 1801 the population stood at less than it had three centuries before, and when the textile trade declined in the face of stiff competition from the Midlands and the North, nothing was available to take its place. The city also missed out on the Industrial Revolution and

the first phase of the railways during the mid-19th century, yet ultimately this meant that much of the traditional fabric and structure of the medieval city was maintained. Salisbury has been able to establish a 21st-century role as a perfect place to live, work and to visit – exactly what Bishop Richard Poore's objective must have been when he founded Salisbury more than 750 years ago.

Salisbury takes pride in its place in English history and is thought to be the only city that celebrates St George's Day, when each April the streets swarm with giants, dragons and damsels in distress, as

ABOVE **Fireworks celebrate the final night of the annual Salisbury International Arts festival.**

RIGHT **St George's Day celebrations pay tribute to England's patron saint.**

lancers and minstrels pay homage to the nation's patron saint. All very appropriate as Salisbury's essential appeal lies in its very Englishness. While Salisbury is proud of its past it is also prepared to invest in its future. More than £22 million has been spent on long-term restoration at the Cathedral; a massive programme that is ongoing.

ABOVE **This picture by Louise Rayner in the Salisbury Museum shows Castle Street around 1870 and graphically portrays the city in Victorian times, with the Cathedral and St Thomas' Church shown clearly at the end of the street.**

RIGHT **Two plaques on the wall of St Ann's Gate in the Close. The Coat of Arms is that of Queen Elizabeth II, commemorating her visit to the city in order to distribute Maundy money.**

IN THE YEAR 1331 KING EDWARD III GRANTED TO THE BISHOP AND THE DEAN AND CHAPTER THE STONE OF THE WALLS OF THE NORMAN CATHEDRAL AT OLD SARUM FOR THE BUILDING OF THE TOWER OF THE CATHEDRAL AND THE WALL WITH BATTLEMENTS ABOUT THE CLOSE.

ABOVE **The Poultry Cross is one of Salisbury's best known landmarks, standing in the heart of the old medieval town. It is the only market cross surviving in the city from the Middle Ages, the top being added in 1852.**

Salisbury Cathedral

The creation of Salisbury Cathedral, over seven centuries ago, represents one of those sublime moments in time when man's vision coincided with favourable circumstances to produce one of the great architectural wonders of the western world.

For some years there had been a frustrated desire to move from the cramped site of the old Norman town in order to build a new cathedral in the valley below, supported by a new town to raise the revenue necessary to maintain such a monumental enterprise. Then a window of opportunity occurred in the turbulent world of early 13th-century England as the visionary and inspirational Richard Poore was elected bishop early in the reign of Henry III, a monarch both keen and extremely generous towards the endowment of new cathedrals. A clear site beckoned

RIGHT **The West Front with its life-size statues of saints and martyrs, kings and bishops, which have been restored to their former glory.**

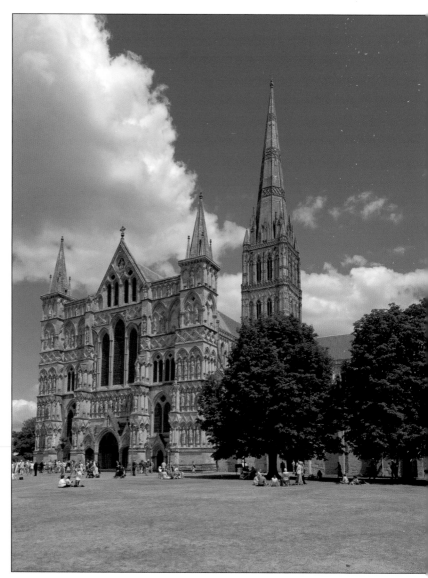

ABOVE The Cloister is the largest cathedral cloister in England. Today its usage remains largely as originally envisaged, a place for contemplation and ceremonial processions.

in the meadows beside the river and the new Gothic architecture possessed all the state of the art technology necessary to make such dreams come true.

Salisbury's Cathedral is unique amongst foremost Gothic cathedrals, in that it was built to a single design in one short, virtually continuous period of time, on what was literally a green-field site. The resulting unity of style, coupled with symmetry of structure, ensured that it became one of Europe's greatest Gothic masterpieces; established in a setting of incomparable beauty, which remains to the present day.

Surprisingly, when Bishop Martival recorded its completion in 1266, the Cathedral lacked its trademark spire, instead there was a detached tower and belfry. By the end of that century however, cathedral spires had become architecturally *de rigueur*, so one of England's best known landmarks came into being, visible for

ABOVE The baroque tomb of Sir Richard Mompesson and his wife Dame Katherine.

LEFT Bishop Osmund completed the original cathedral at Old Sarum. His tomb was one of three containing the remains of bishops brought down and installed in the new cathedral, thereby maintaining a unique connection between Old and New Sarum.

many miles around, guiding visitors towards the city of Salisbury and its great Cathedral.

The medieval church was a stage on which to perform religious ceremony, the cathedral being the ultimate theatre where educated clergy conveyed the word of God to a largely illiterate congregation through a compelling mixture of light, sound and colourful procession. In modern times Salisbury Cathedral is an eloquent reminder of both why and how a great Gothic cathedral was conceived as a sophisticated, highly skilful blend of architecture, engineering and craftsmanship of the highest order – masons, carpenters, glaziers and other skilled workers using their own personal interpretation to enrich the fabric in a gloriously uninhibited manner. Today

Salisbury's cathedral was the brainchild of Bishop Richard Poore, the illegitimate son of the bishop of nearby Winchester. Poore was a charismatic mixture of 13th-century cleric: a scholarly, articulate, man of vision, and 20th-century property developer: shrewd, dynamic and highly persuasive. Unlike the other medieval bishops buried here, Poore does not have an impressive tomb in the nave, his memorial is the Cathedral itself, one of England's greatest Gothic achievements.

LEFT As there is no choir screen, the interior of the Cathedral allows an uninterrupted view along its entire length. The exquisite Salisbury Font, installed in 2008, was designed by William Pye to combine both movement and stillness.

the Dean and Chapter retains this time-honoured tradition, continuing to employ resident stonemasons, wood carvers and glaziers, whilst also making extensive use of embroiderers.

Seven centuries ago medieval engineering was exploring the frontiers of technology without the benefit of computers or other electronic or mechanical gadgetry. Salisbury's famous tower and spire is 6,500 tonnes of masonry supported by four slender columns resting on shallow foundations of gravel and rubble. Standing at the crossing in the Cathedral and looking upward at the distorted columns might convey a degree of alarm, yet they have remained like this for many centuries.

Alongside the Cathedral stands the Chapter House, where the Dean and Chapter once met to conduct Cathedral business. It is an architectural gem in its own right with a distinctive fan vaulted ceiling rising from a single slender column – some scholars consider it superior to the Chapter House at Westminster Abbey. It contains an intricately carved

13th-century frieze depicting scenes from the Old Testament and also one of the nation's most important historical documents: one of only four surviving copies of the Magna Carta, supervised by Elias of Dereham, the man considered by some to be the true architect of the Cathedral.

ABOVE **The choir stalls contain superbly carved heads of both human and animal forms, some dating from the end of the 19th century, others dating back to the Cathedral's origins in the 13th century.**

ABOVE LEFT **In 1980, Yehudi Menuhin unveiled the Prisoners of Conscience window. The inspiration was that of the Dean of the time, Sydney Evans, and was created by French glazier Gabriel Loire of Chartres.**

LEFT **This glass prism was etched with images of the Cathedral by Laurence Whistler as a memorial to his artist brother Rex, who died in France during World War II.**

The Close

Inside the archway of the North Gate,
city centre hustle and bustle fades
into the altogether quieter world
of the Close. Springy turf, towering
chestnuts, fruit trees in the gardens, a
little piece of country come to town.
This is the largest Close in England,
dating back to the foundation of
the Cathedral in the 13th century
when Bishop Richard Poore began
to install his palace and commanded
his canons to build homes for them-
selves and their servants around
the huge construction site that
surrounded the Cathedral more than
seven centuries ago.

Many of the houses in the Close
originate from those distant days and
some still retain distinctive traces
of their medieval origins. Many
more, like those on the West Walk
were re-built in that sublime period
of architecture that evolved in the
heady days following the Restoration,
a glorious era for Salisbury when
Charles II, Sir Christopher Wren and

ABOVE **The Close is
entered from the city
centre via North Gate,
which was originally
constructed in the
mid-14th century
at the same time as
the massive stone
walls which enclosed
the Close, using
stone taken from the
ruins of Old Sarum
Cathedral outside the
city. The statue is that
of King Edward VII.**

RIGHT **The Bishop's
Palace, now the
Cathedral School.
Bishops of Salisbury
lived here until 1946.**

RIGHT **Choristers Green is located on the north side of the Close. Mompesson House was built in 1701 by Charles Mompesson, a local MP, whilst next door Hungerford Chantry is a re-built medieval chantry alongside Hemyngsby, named after Alexander Hemyngsby, the Choir School's first recorded warden.**

The nation's best known architect, Sir Christopher Wren, was born in 1632 in the little village of East Knoyle, just west of Salisbury. When Bishop Ward became concerned about the state of the Cathedral, he sought advice from Wren, formerly Professor of Astronomy at the University of Oxford. Wren had no formal architectural training, but was a mathematician with an ability to draw. He lived to the age of 90 and is buried in his masterpiece, St Paul's in London.

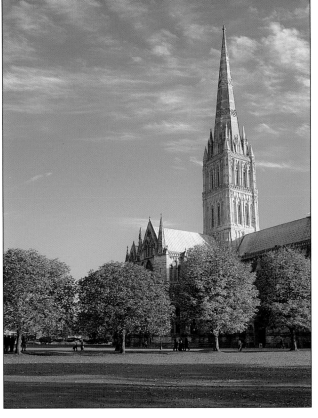

LEFT **The spire, an architectural icon of western Europe, stands more than 400ft (122m) high, a brilliant feat of medieval engineering and the tallest spire in England, largely because taller ones, such as Lincoln Minster's, have come tumbling down. Salisbury's tower and spire survives despite having been struck by lightning on a number of occasions. The original detached tower and belfry was demolished by James Wyatt in the late 18th century.**

Samuel Pepys walked in the Close and the rich and famous came to live there.

Another group of stylish houses which date from the early 18th century lie on the northern end of the Close in the exquisite little square at the end of the short lane running down from North Gate, known as Chorister's Green. Even in the height of summer the Green remains a serene oasis surrounded by lime trees and buildings depicting English architecture at its very best.

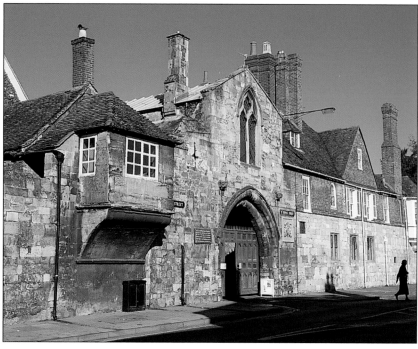

The 18th-century writer, Henry Fielding, lived alongside St Ann's Gate. He was like one of the characters in his rumbustious novels, such as *Tom Jones*, partly written in Salisbury. His long suffering neighbours complained of 'wild extravagances and gorgeous velvet suits.' Fielding, however, possessed a deep sense of social justice and was also a magistrate for Westminster. When he died in Lisbon aged only 47, he had done much to establish the novel as the most popular form in English literature.

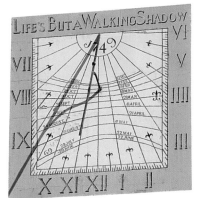

RIGHT This sundial on the wall of Malmesbury House shows the old Julian calendar used before the present day version. The Julian calendar managed to lose 11 days over the years, the adjustment introduced in 1752 meant that the date went from 2nd September to 14th in one day.

THIS IS LIFE ETERNAL THAT THEY MAY KNOW THEE THE ONLY TRUE GOD. AND JESUS CHRIST. WHOM THOU HAST SENT.
ST JOHN. CHAPTER 17. VERSE 3.

North Walk runs down to St Ann's Gate and Malmesbury House, a former 13th-century canonry that was re-built in 1704 by the father of James 'Hermes' Harris, who acquired his nickname by writing a highly acclaimed treatise on ancient philosophy with that title. Harris was an energetic character with a dazzling circle of friends including Dr Samuel Johnson, the famous diarist James Boswell, Henry Fielding, the fun-loving author of *Tom Jones*, portrait painter Sir Joshua Reynolds and the theatrical impresario David Garrick. He was also an avid admirer of the composer Handel, who is said to have performed his first English concert in a room above St Ann's Gate, which leads out of the eastern end of the Close beyond Malmesbury House, whilst Fielding conducted riotous parties next door. The tradition of well-known people living in the Close is maintained to modern times: former Prime Minister Sir Edward Heath lived at Arundells until 2005 and the house is now open to the public for guided tours.

Today all these elegant houses face the Cathedral across immaculately cut turf, yet this was not always the case; indeed the whole area was a muddy water-logged graveyard until the arrival of the architect James Wyatt in the 19th century. 'Salisbury is the sink

LEFT St Ann's Gate is one of the three medieval gates in the Close, which are locked at night.

LEFT The College of Matrons is an almshouse founded for the widows of the clergy in 1682 by the kindly and eccentric bishop, Dr Seth Ward, and is said by some to be the work of Sir Christopher Wren.

of Wiltshire, the Close is the sink of Salisbury', the Elizabethan antiquary, John Leland had once scoffed. 'Wrecker' Wyatt is rightly criticised for his insensitive alterations to the cathedral's interior, yet he was also responsible for removing the tombstones and draining the swamp, thereby creating the beautiful setting for the Cathedral that can be seen today.

LEFT In late afternoon the Cathedral spire casts a long shadow towards the north-east corner of the Close.

BELOW The Walking Madonna, Dame Elizabeth Frink's striking sculpture, seemingly strides away from the North Porch across the Close towards the North Gate.

BELOW Arundells was a medieval house rebuilt in the 18th century. It is rumoured that a 16th-century canon was dispossessed whilst living here when caught practising sorcery.

Begin at the Guildhall in the Market Square, proceed down an alleyway running alongside the Guildhall into Butcher Row (*left*), turning right along one of Salisbury's oldest thoroughfares leading to the **Poultry Cross** (p.7). Opposite is **The Haunch of Venison** (p.23), one of the city's many surviving medieval inns. Cross over Minster Street to Silver Street, on the right is St Thomas Square containing the exquisite church dedicated to **Thomas à Becket** (pp.21,23). Continue into Bridge Street taking the pathway on your left running alongside the River Avon as far as Crane Bridge. Crossing the bridge affords a lovely view of the river and the back of Church House (*right*). Return into Crane street over the bridge and almost at once an archway on the right leads into the secluded courtyard of the medieval Church House, successively private dwelling, city workhouse and Cathedral Diocesan Office. At the junction of Crane Street and High Street turn right under **North Gate** (p.12) into the Close, past the stylish **College of Matrons** (p.15), still a residence for clergy widows. On the right are **Chorister's Green** (p.13) and

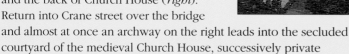

a series of graceful 18th-century houses such as **Mompesson House** (pp.13, 19), Hungerford Chantry, Hemyngsby (*above*), Wren Hall and Braybrooke. Continue along West Walk past the line of exceptionally beautiful buildings like **Myles Place** (p.6) and the Walton Canory, which face the Cathedral across close-cropped turf. At the far end of the Close turn left out of Harnham Gate (otherwise known

as South Gate) into **De Vaux Place** (p.5), once the location of the House of the Valley of Scholars. Turn right down St Nicholas Road past **St Nicholas Hospital** (p.21), a medieval almshouse, and on to Aylesware Bridge (*above*), originally built by Bishop Bingham

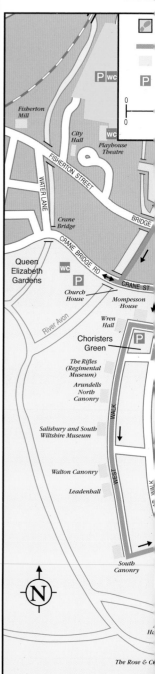

A walk

This walk starts in the heart most interesting sites. The ro and ta

Fisherton Mill

City Hall

Playhouse Theatre

Crane Bridge

BRIDGE

Queen Elizabeth Gardens

Church House

Mompesson House

CRANE ST

Wren Hall

Choristers Green

The Rifles (Regimental Museum)

Arundells North Canonry

Salisbury and South Wiltshire Museum

Walton Canonry

Leadenhall

South Canonry

N

The Rose & C

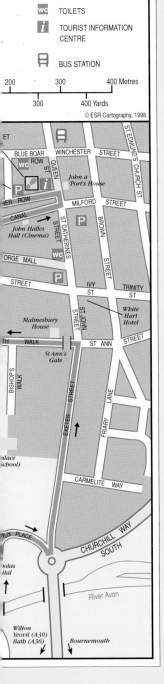

in about 1244. There is a lovely view downstream, whilst upstream lies the **Rose and Crown** (*below*) (p.23), a fine half-timbered 14th-century inn, whose riverside garden affords a superb view of the Cathedral spire across the meadows. Return along St Nicholas Road turning right and immediately left into Exeter Street beside the high wall built in the early 14th century to protect the Close. At the end of Exeter Street, **St Ann's Gate** (pp.7, 14) leads back into the Close along North Walk. Note the intriguing sundial on the wall of the 18th-century **Malmesbury House** (pp.14, 20). Along North Walk lies Sarum College (*below*), Bishop Wordsworth's School and the medieval house of Aula le Stage. At the end of North Walk turn right towards North Gate. The statue above the arch is of Edward VII (*below right*).

The houses on the left are considerably older than the 17th-century College of Matron's opposite. Continue into High Street, note the three attractive half-timbered 14th-century houses on the left beyond North Gate, whilst further along on the right is the entrance to the Old George Mall. Turn right into New Canal, which had an open watercourse

running down its centre until the last century. Half way down on the right is John Halle's Hall (*below left*), originally the home of a wealthy 15th-century merchant, today surely England's most unusual cinema. At the end of New Canal turn left into Queen Street past the black and white, **John a 'Port's house** (p.20) beyond which the road opens up into the Market Square and the Guildhall.

Museums and historic buildings

'Salisbury Museum is outstanding, I urge you to go there at once', enthuses Bill Bryson in his highly entertaining book, *Notes from a Small Island.* It is a richly deserved accolade, the museum being considerably larger than it initially appears from the outside, with 15 rooms spread over two floors housing an eclectic and absorbing display of exhibits that are consistently being added to, whilst individual specialist exhibitions are mounted on a regular basis.

Objects on view range from the scholarly to the rather sinister – two exhibits which attract most attention being a graphic re-construction of a neolithic grave and a mummified rat discovered in the 13th-century Earl

LEFT **One of the Five Senses, this one depicting hearing, unique ceramic figures created at Bow in the mid-18th century. Salisbury Museum has a rare example of a complete set in mint condition.**

BELOW **The King's House. This mellow brick building in the Close now houses the excellent Salisbury and South Wiltshire Museum.**

of Salisbury's tomb in the nearby Cathedral. 'Liked the skeleton and the rat. Wow!' reads an enthusiastic entry in the visitors' book. The museum also contains a number of Turner's

famous watercolours, 600 pieces of recently redesigned Wedgwood pottery and a Stonehenge gallery, whilst the Pitt-Rivers collection of archaeological and old-style agricultural objects is a brilliant museum within a museum.

A noteworthy museum in the Close is The Rifles (Berkshire and Wiltshire Museum) once used as a clothing storehouse by successive bishops, hence the name. Additionally three fine early 18th-century houses stand in the Close, Mompesson House, Malmesbury House (not open to the public) and Arundells.

Mompesson House featured in the award winning film *Sense and Sensibility*. The house, built in 1701, has magnificent plasterwork

ABOVE **The Rifles Museum is housed in a building known as The Wardrobe.**

BELOW **Owned by the National Trust, Mompesson House is a gracious Queen Anne house with a magnificent**

***Magnolia grandiflora* energetically climbing up its cool grey stone façade.**

ABOVE **A present-day Salisbury giant, successor of the ancient Tailor's Guild giant now kept in Salisbury Museum.**

ABOVE AND ABOVE RIGHT **Malmesbury House has an interior which is richly Rococo. The façade is said to have been executed by John Fort, one of Sir Christopher Wren's master builders.**

and a fine oak staircase added in the 1740s. As well as good quality period furniture, the house contains the Turnbull Collection of English 18th-century drinking glasses. Outside, the walled garden has traditional herbaceous borders.

The central area of Salisbury beyond the Close is equally rich in buildings originating from the Middle Ages. Fine churches, wealthy merchants' houses, ancient inns and a number of almshouses, which still provide care and accommodation for the elderly, just as they did many centuries ago. **Joiners' Hall** in St Ann Street, once an ancient guild hall, has unusual wooden gargoyles on its 17th-century façade, whilst relics of **Shoemakers' Hall** now form part of the **Pheasant Inn** in Salt Lane. On the corner of New Street and High Street is the **Mitre House**, said to occupy the site of Salisbury's first dwelling place, where Bishop Poore lodged whilst his palace was under construction. Each new bishop still dresses here for his enthronement, before proceeding in joyful procession with the Dean and Chapter across the Close to the Cathedral.

Much of the original street plan of the city survives from medieval times, displaying names such as Blue Boar Row, New Canal and Pennyfarthing Lane, so called because the masons living there apparently once downed tools until their wages were raised

ABOVE **John a 'Port's House, reputedly the home of John a 'Port, a powerful city merchant who was six times Mayor of Salisbury.**

20

ABOVE A 14th-century, half-timbered house in the High Street.

RIGHT Wealthy city merchants financed the development of St Thomas' Church. The magnificent 15th-century interior features the nation's largest 'doom' painting depicting The Last Judgement.

When the splendidly named Lieut.-General Augustus Henry Lane-Fox Pitt-Rivers retired from active service, he embarked on a new career as an archaeologist, going on to become the nation's first ever Inspector of Ancient Monuments. Pitt-Rivers was an avid collector of ethnographic objects, now exhibited in the Salisbury and South Wiltshire Museum and the Pitt-Rivers Museum in Oxford.

to that amount! Two original stone bridges still exist over the River Avon, **Crane Bridge** and **Ayleswade Bridge**, otherwise known as Harnham Bridge, built by Bishop Bingham in 1244, alongside the earlier river-crossing of Aegel's Ford. Nearby, just south of the Close, a group of students from Oxford established the House of the Valley of Scholars in 1261. For a while it seemed likely that a new university might be conceived, but sadly the students returned to Oxford. Today the only sign of this missed opportunity is a carved angel holding the Oxford University Coat of Arms on the wall of **De Vaux House**. 'Sic transit gloria mundi', as the scholars might have said!

LEFT The Hospital of St Nicholas is one of several almshouses in Salisbury dating from the 13th century. Located in St Nicholas Road close to Ayleswade Bridge, parts of the two buildings that face each other across a courtyard date back to the first years of the city and were featured in Anthony Trollope's *Barchester Chronicles*.

Shopping and entertainment

Salisbury has excellent shopping facilities with outlets varying from national retailers to small specialist shops. The Park and Ride sites at **The Beehive**, **London Road**, **Wilton**, **Britford** and **Petersfinger** give easy access to the city centre. Many of the shops are in three modern malls: the **Maltings**, sited around a former flour mill by the river, the **Cross Keys Centre** by the market square and the **Old George Mall**, behind the façade of the old medieval George Inn in the High Street.

Fisherton Mill, an old grain mill in Fisherton Street, houses a Design and Contemporary Craft emporium, with outdoors exhibitions, workshops and fine arts galleries.

This upsurge in modern commercial activity has not detracted from the traditional market which continues to operate twice a week as it has done since 1315, while a three-storey flea market is situated in Catherine Street.

Nor has the arrival of new restaurants and pavement cafés in the city centre endangered the numerous half-timbered inns that flourish just as they did in the Middle Ages.

Wilton Shopping Village, a few miles away, offers leading brands at discount prices in factory outlet shops.

Those who like a flutter on the horses will enjoy a day at **Salisbury Racecourse** on the edge of the city.

There's first-class entertainment at **Salisbury Playhouse** where an excellent repertory company performs a varied programme and at the **City Hall** which offers national touring shows as well as exhibitions, lectures and local amateur shows. The highlight of the year is the Salisbury International Arts Festival when the city hosts two weeks of concerts, plays and exhibitions together with a galaxy of other cultural activities.

RIGHT **Salisbury's prosperity was founded on the wool trade. One of its mills was at Harnham, across the water meadows and an easy walk from the city centre. It remained a working mill well into the 20th century and is now an inn.**

RIGHT **The Maltings. Now a restaurant, the Bishop's Mill on the river was once a flour mill and together with several commercial malthouses built in the 19th century it now forms part of a modern shopping mall.**

LEFT A colourful pavement café located in the sheltered surroundings of St Thomas' Square beside the medieval church of St Thomas à Becket.

BELOW The Rose and Crown with its decorative inn sign can be found near Harnham Bridge.

RIGHT The Haunch of Venison. Behind glass in the upstairs bar is the ghoulish sight of the mummified hand of an unfortunate 18th-century card player apparently caught cheating, bringing a new meaning to the term, 'dealt a bad hand'.

FAR RIGHT Actors on stage at Salisbury Playhouse in *The Game of Love and Chance*.

Stonehenge – a long life

It all began a very long time ago in the late neolithic period around 3000 BC, with the construction of a huge circular ditch and earth bank, using picks made from deer's antlers and primitive wooden shovels. Work continued through a series of distinctive phases until suddenly, around 1600 BC, this extraordinary engineering feat was considered to be complete. Thereafter no further work was undertaken and by the time the Romans arrived in Britain, Stonehenge was an abandoned and empty ruin.

Even today the reason for its very existence remains shrouded in mystery, its precise purpose a matter of pure speculation. Modern science might indicate when and how Stonehenge was built but why, or even by whom, continues to be an elusive enigma.

Some say Merlin transported this ring of stones from Ireland using supernatural powers. Inigo Jones was convinced that the Romans were responsible. The antiquarians John Aubrey and William Stukeley favoured the Druids, whilst more recently Dr Aubrey Burl, a leading British pre-historian, suggested that Stonehenge was probably built by the French.

Theories explaining Stonehenge's function are equally exotic, ranging from a place of ritual human sacrifice to a very early astronomical observatory. The medieval monk Geoffrey of Monmouth felt that Stonehenge was a memorial to ancient British warriors slain by the Saxons, while Professors Gerald Hawkins and Fred Hoyle infuriated the archaeologists by arguing that Stonehenge was really a neolithic

RIGHT **This general plan of Stonehenge clearly indicates the key features including the remains of the ditch, circle and horseshoe. The dotted line indicates the alignment of the midsummer sunrise that continues to be celebrated by modern day druids. The Aubrey Holes were originally discovered by John Aubrey whilst the Heel Stone featured in a folk tale about a monk hit on his heel by a stone hurled by the Devil.**

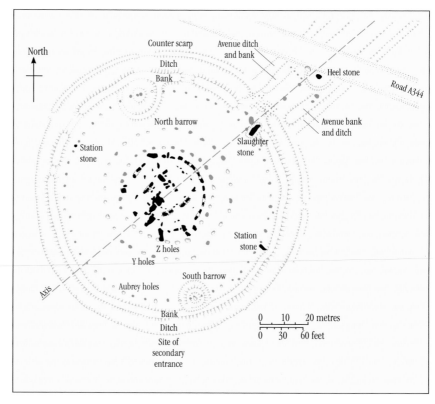

NSET **Stonehenge
rom the east on a
erfect winter's day,
ust as the ancient
ravellers would have
een it as they crossed
he isolated frozen
wastes of Salisbury
Plain in centuries
gone by.**

computer, utilising a complex
network of solar and lunar
alignments to predict eclipses and
other heavenly events.

The most remarkable fact however,
is that Stonehenge has survived the
ravages of time and continues to
intrigue, fascinate and delight the
hundreds of thousands of visitors
that come each year to this desolate
part of Salisbury Plain to gaze at

As the sun sinks
behind the sarsens
memory fades
o myth, fantasy
becomes reality
and all things seem
possible.

something which has no known equivalent anywhere else in the world.

The word 'Stonehenge' probably derives from the Saxon 'Stanhengist' or 'place of the hanging stones'. It is the lintels atop the huge uprights that make Stonehenge so unique, setting it apart from other great prehistoric monuments such as nearby Avebury, Callanish off the west coast of Scotland, or Carnac in Brittany, which, though dubbed 'the French Stonehenge', lacks the distinctive lintels.

Scholars are more certain about the construction of Stonehenge than virtually any other aspect of this World Heritage Site. Carbon dating has established the various building periods, though ever-more sophisticated techniques tend to push these back even further towards the edge of time. The smaller blue stones, which replaced the original timber setting around 2600 BC, were transported from the Preseli Mountains, along the south coast of Wales on rafts, then up river to Amesbury to be manhandled with rollers and sledges to the Stonehenge site, a total distance of nearly 250 miles (402km). The sarsens, huge sandstone boulders each weighing 25 tonnes, were dragged over from the Marlborough Downs some 20 miles

ABOVE **Thomas Rowlandson's 'Stone'enge on Salisbury Plain', now in the Salisbury and South Wiltshire Museum, was drawn in about 1784 in the artist's typically rumbustious style. The stones appear about to collapse in a drunken stupor.**

(32km) to the north. Thirty uprights capped by a continuous line of curved lintels formed the stone circle and the central horseshoe containing the Altar Stone. The principal entrance was from the north-east marked by three portal stones; today just one, the so-called 'Slaughter Stone', still exists, lying on its side. Outside the entrance the Heel Stone marks the alignment of the mid-summer sunrise whilst two other Station Stones remain from a group of four, a quartet which once indicated other astrological alignments including midwinter sunset and other lunar cycles.

The standing stones were smoothed and shaped, and prehistoric carvings can be detected on their surface. The lintels are held together by mortice and tenon joints which are locked end to end by tongue and groove. The foundation pits are quite shallow and the upright stones were held merely by impacted chalk and small stones, and yet a remarkable number have stayed upright. It is interesting to note that approximately a third of each stone is actually under the surface of the ground, helping to keep it standing, so that what is seen is actually only two thirds of the total of each stone.

Many aspects of Stonehenge remain a matter of debate, an indisputable fact, however, is that it represents one of the greatest feats of all time. As the 12th-century cleric Henry of Huntingdon marvelled, 'stones of wonderful size have been erected after the manner of doorways and no-one can conceive how such great stones have been so raised aloft or why they were built there'.

ABOVE **William Stukely, the pioneering 17th-century antiquary, invented the term 'trilithon', Greek for 'three stones', to describe two uprights surmounted by a horizontal lintel. The tallest upright is 22 ft (7m) high and weighs 45 tonnes.**

Around Salisbury and Stonehenge

Wiltshire is a county best known for Salisbury Cathedral and Stonehenge, yet around these two world-famous landmarks lies countryside of infinitely varied delight: lush pasture, trout streams trickling gently through deeply wooded valleys, then the windswept uplands of Salisbury Plain, which has the largest collection of neolithic and Bronze Age remains to be found anywhere in the British Isles.

The area has never experienced the dubious pleasures of modern industrialisation, but remains primarily agricultural; close-knit farming communities retaining traditional values. There are villages with names such as Fonthill Bishop, Monkton Deverill, Codford St Peter and Winterbourne Gunner. Many of the cottages are thatched; those in the Wylye valley, west of Salisbury, built in the distinctive chequers of local stone and knapped flint. Timeless and unhurried, it is a place to explore and savour slowly.

The enormous megalithic monument of **Avebury** stands on the northern fringes of Salisbury Plain: it is a complex arrangement of stone circles and earthworks with processional avenues radiating out across the countryside. Closer to Salisbury is the city's predecessor, **Old Sarum**, a great Iron Age hillfort successively occupied by the Romans, Saxons and Normans, who built a royal castle and cathedral here. Over the centuries its population dwindled to a handful of people who, until the Reform Act of 1832, still elected their own MP, making Old Sarum synonymous with the term 'Rotten Borough'.

The county contains two of England's finest Renaissance houses, Wilton and Longleat, together with several of the nation's loveliest gardens. **Wilton House** has been the home of the Earls of Pembroke since the reign of Henry VIII. Built on the site of an abbey, the house played host to a circle of courtly poets in the Elizabethan era, including the Countess of Pembroke's brother, Sir Philip Sidney. Damaged by fire in 1647 it was restored to the designs of Inigo Jones. **Longleat House**, set within an elegant landscape designed by Capability Brown, was begun in 1568 by an ancestor of the present owner, the Marquess of Bath. Its

ABOVE **One of the ancient stones at Avebury.**

BELOW **The outline of the old cathedral at Old Sarum.**

BELOW RIGHT **Wilton House is beautifully sited by the River Nadder with a fine Palladian bridge and an interior which contains a dazzling range of treasures.**

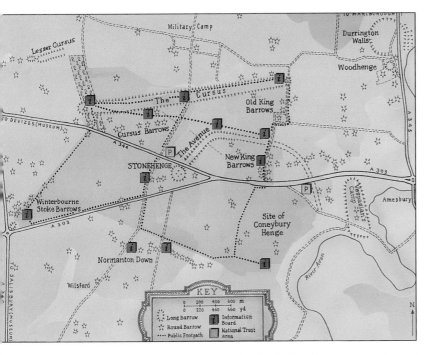

FAR LEFT **The
magnificent orangery
at Longleat.**

LEFT **Heale House,
which dates from the
16th century, once
gave refuge to Charles
II whilst fleeing
Cromwell's troops
after the Battle of
Worcester.**

BELOW **Stourhead
has gardens of
exceptional beauty
around a huge lake in
a deep valley.**

amous Safari Park is one of the most
ascinating attractions in the region.

The gardens at **Heale House** to
he north of Salisbury are a rare
delight in a glorious unspoilt part
of the Wiltshire countryside. Just
ixteen miles west of Stonehenge is
Stourhead, with impressive gardens
aid out in the late 18th century. The
estate also contains a 160ft (48m) high
olly known as King Alfred's Tower,
offering views over three counties.

Further information

Details are correct at the time of writing but may be changed.

Arundells
A fine 18th-century house, formerly the home of Sir Edward Heath.
59 Cathedral Close, Salisbury. Open for guided tours Mar–Oct Sat, Mon–Weds, 11–5. (Tel booking line open 11–3 daily except Thur and Sun 01722 326546.) www.arundells.org/

Avebury
One of the most important megalithic monuments in Europe.
Avebury, nr Marlborough (tel 01672 539250). Open all year from 10am. National Trust. Admission free. www.nationaltrust.org.uk/avebury

City Hall
Entertainment thoughout the year to suit all tastes in this multi-function venue. Also hosts private events.
Malthouse Lane (tel 01722 434434, info 01722 434726). www.cityhallsalisbury.co.uk

Heale House Garden and Plant Centre
The first winner of the Christie's/Historic Houses Association Garden of the Year award.
Middle Woodford (tel 01722 782504). Gardens and plant centre open Feb-Oct Wed–Sun and Bank Holiday Mondays 10–5. Admission charge. www.healegarden.co.uk

Larmer Tree Victorian Pleasure Gardens
11-acre gardens laid out by General Pitt Rivers in 1880.
Tollard Royal (tel 01725 516228). Open Easter–late Sept Sun–Thur 11–4.30. Tea rooms 11–5 Sun. Admission charge. www.larmertreegardens.co.uk

ABOVE **Longleat House before the lake or 'long lete' from which the house derives its name.**

Longleat
The Marquess of Bath's Elizabethan stately home. Superb gardens, grounds, safari park and many other attractions.
Nr Warminster (tel 01985 844400). All attractions open daily Apr–Oct 10–4 (house open until 5pm). Gardens and house open daily. Admission charge. www.longleat.co.uk

Mompesson House
A definitive example of a Queen Anne town house.
The Close (tel 01722 335659). Open mid-Mar–end Oct 11–5 except Thu and Fri. National Trust. Admission charge for non-members. www. nationaltrust.org.uk/ mompesson-house

Rockbourne Roman Villa
The remains of the largest known Roman villa in the area.
Rockbourne, Fordingbridge (tel 0845 603 5635). Open Apr–Sep Thu, Fri, Sun 11-4. Admission charge.

Old Sarum
The evocative ruins of the first settlement of Salisbury.
Castle Road (tel 01722 335398). Open daily Mar, Oct 10–4, Apr–Jun, Sep 10–5; Jul, Aug 9–6; Nov–Feb 10-3. English Heritage. Admission charge for non-members.

The Rifles (Berkshire and Wiltshire) Museum
The Close (tel 01722 419419). Open Apr–Oct daily 10–5; Mar 10–5., closed Sun. Admission charge. www.thewardrobe.co.uk

Salisbury and South Wiltshire Museum
An award-winning museum of considerable interest.
The King's House, The Close (tel 01722 332151). Open all year Mon–Sat 10–5, Sun in Jun–Sep 12–5. Admission charge. www.salisburymuseum.org.uk

Salisbury Arts Centre
A range of performing and visual arts in a former church.
Bedwin Street (tel 01722 321744, box office tel 01722 321744). Open Tue–Sat 10–4. Box office open on performance nights. www.salisburyartscentre.co.uk

ABOVE **In late summer Salisbury Plain is a landscape of red and yellow and green, the red of poppies and the yellow of rape.**